$=$

$\dfrac{A}{T}$

The Echo Gate

Also by Michael Longley

No Continuing City
(Poems 1963 — 68)

An Exploded View
(Poems 1968 — 72)

Man Lying on a Wall
(Poems 1972 — 75)

as editor

Causeway
(The Arts in Ulster)

Under the Moon: Over the Stars
(Children's Verse)

The Echo Gate
Poems 1975-79

Michael Longley

Secker & Warburg · London

First published in England 1979 by
Martin Secker & Warburg Limited
54 Poland Street, London W1V 3DF

Copyright © Michael Longley 1979

436 25680 0

Printed and bound in Great Britain by
REDWOOD BURN LIMITED
Trowbridge & Esher

For Michael Allen & Paul Muldoon

I have heard of an island
With only one house on it.
The gulls are at home there.
Our perpetual absence
Is a way of leaving
All the eggs unbroken
That litter the ground
Right up to its doorstep.

Acknowledgements

Some of these poems have appeared previously in *Antaeus, Belfast Telegraph, Encounter, Fortnight, Gown, Hibernia, Honest Ulsterman, Irish Press, Irish Times, New Poems, New Poetry, New Review, New Statesman, Poetry Review, Stone Ferry Review, Thames Poetry, Times Literary Supplement*; and on BBC2 TV, Radio Ulster, Radio 3 and Radio Telefis Eireann.

Contents

Obsequies 9
Oliver Plunkett 10
Wreaths 12
Last Requests 14
Second Sight 15
Home Ground 16
Architecture 17
The Echo Gate 18
Ash Keys 19
Frozen Rain 20
Thaw 21
Spring Tide 22
Lore 24
On Hearing Irish Spoken 26
Mayo Monologues 27
Entomology 31
Botany 32
Bog Cotton 33
The War Poets 34
Peace 35
Sulpicia 38
Florence Nightingale 39
Grace Darling 40
Metamorphoses 41
Mountain Swim 42
On Mweelrea 43
Meniscus 44
The Linen Industry 45
Martinmas 46
Household Hints 47
The Rag Trade 48
Dead Men's Fingers 49
The Barber's Wife 50
Self-portrait 51
Codicils 52
Notes 53

Obsequies

They are proof-reading my obituary now
As I fall asleep in formalin and float
Just below the surface of death, mute
At the centre of my long obsequies.

Were they to queue up to hear me breathing
The chemicals, then head over heels
All my lovers would fall in love again,
For I am a big fish in the aquarium,

A saint whose bits and pieces separate
Into a dozen ceremonies, pyres
For hands that bedded down like Gandhi
With the untouchables, funerals for feet.

They have set my eyes like two diamonds
In the black velvet of another's head,
Bartered silver, gold from knuckle and tooth
To purchase some sustenance for the needy.

Meanwhile, back at the dissecting theatre,
Part of me waits to find in sinks and basins
A final ocean, tears, water from the tap,
Superstitious rivers to take me there.

Oliver Plunkett

1.   His Soul

When they cut off his head, the long whiskers
Went on growing, as if to fledge his soul
And facilitate its gradual departure.

So much of him was concentrated there
That, quite without his realizing it,
They divided the body into four.

It amounted to more than a withdrawal
When the last drop of moisture had dispersed
And one by one the hairs fell from his chin,

For the fatty brain was shrivelling as well,
Leaving around itself enormous spaces
And accommodation for the likes of him.

His own leathery shrine, he seems to be
Refracting the gleam in his father's eye
Like a shattered mirror in a handbag.

2.   His Head

This is the end of the body that thinks
And says things, says things as the body does —
Kisses, belches, sighs — while making room for
The words of wisdom and the testimonies.

And these are a baby's features, a child's
Expression condensing on the plate glass,
The specimen suspended in its bottle
At eye level between shelf and shelf.

His head looks out from the tiny coffin
As though his body were crouching there
Inside the altar, a magician
Who is in charge of this conjuring trick,

Or an astronaut trapped by his oxygen
And eager to float upwards to the ceiling
Away from the gravitational pull
Of his arms and legs which are very old.

Your own face is reflected by the casket
And this is anybody's head in a room
Except that the walls are all windows and
He has written his name over the glass.

3.   His Body

Trying to estimate what height he was
Keeps the soul awake, like the pea under
The heap of mattresses under the princess.

And now that they've turned him into a saint
Even a fly buzzing about the roof space
Must affect the balance of his mind.

His thigh bones and shoulder blades are scales
That a speck of dust could tilt, making him
Walk with a limp or become a hunchback.

He has been buried under the fingernails
Of his executioners, until they too fade
Like the lightning flash of their instruments.

There accompanies him around the cathedral
Enough silence to register the noise
Of the hairs on arms and legs expiring.

Wreaths

The Civil Servant

He was preparing an Ulster fry for breakfast
When someone walked into the kitchen and shot him:
A bullet entered his mouth and pierced his skull,
The books he had read, the music he could play.

He lay in his dressing gown and pyjamas
While they dusted the dresser for fingerprints
And then shuffled backwards across the garden
With notebooks, cameras and measuring tapes.

They rolled him up like a red carpet and left
Only a bullet hole in the cutlery drawer:
Later his widow took a hammer and chisel
And removed the black keys' from his piano.

The Greengrocer

He ran a good shop, and he died
Serving even the death-dealers
Who found him busy as usual
Behind the counter, organised
With holly wreaths for Christmas,
Fir trees on the pavement outside.

Astrologers or three wise men
Who may shortly be setting out
For a small house up the Shankill
Or the Falls, should pause on their way
To buy gifts at Jim Gibson's shop,
Dates and chestnuts and tangerines.

The Linen Workers

Christ's teeth ascended with him into heaven:
Through a cavity in one of his molars
The wind whistles: he is fastened for ever
By his exposed canines to a wintry sky.

I am blinded by the blaze of that smile
And by the memory of my father's false teeth
Brimming in their tumbler: thèy wore bubbles
And, outside of his body, a deadly grin.

When they massacred the ten linen workers
There fell on the road beside them spectacles,
Wallets, small change, and a set of dentures:
Blood, food particles, the bread, the wine.

Before I can bury my father once again
I must polish the spectacles, balance them
Upon his nose, fill his pockets with money
And into his dead mouth slip the set of teeth.

Last Requests

1

Your batman thought you were buried alive,
Left you for dead and stole your pocket watch
And cigarette case, all he could salvage
From the grave you so nearly had to share
With an unexploded shell. But your lungs
Surfaced to take a long remembered drag,
Heart contradicting as an epitaph
The two initials you had scratched on gold.

2

I thought you blew a kiss before you died,
But the bony fingers that waved to and fro
Were asking for a Woodbine, the last request
Of many soldiers in your company,
The brand you chose to smoke for forty years
Thoughtfully, each one like a sacrament.
I who brought peppermints and grapes only
Couldn't reach you through the oxygen tent.

Second Sight

My father's mother had the second sight.
Flanders began at the kitchen window —
The mangle rusting in No Man's Land, gas
Turning the antimacassars yellow
When it blew the wrong way from the salient.

In bandages, on crutches, reaching home
Before his letters, my father used to find
The front door on the latch, his bed airing.
'I watched my son going over the top.
He was carrying flowers out of the smoke.'

I have brought the *Pocket Guide to London,*
My *Map of the Underground,* an address —
A lover looking for somewhere to live,
A ghost among ghosts of aunts and uncles
Who crowd around me to give directions.

Where is my father's house, where my father?
If I could walk in on my grandmother
She'd see right through me and the hallway
And the miles of cloud and sky to Ireland.
'You have crossed the water to visit me.'

Home Ground

1
for S.H.

This was your home ground, comings and goings
When the sand martins collected in flight
Feathers and straw for untidy chambers
Or swooped up to kiss each tiny darkness,
Five white eggs changing to five white chins:

Childhood, and your townland poor enough
For gentians, fairy flax, wild strawberries
And the anxious lapwing that settled there,
Its vocal chords a grass blade stretched
Between your thumbs and blown to tatters.

2
for P.M.

When they landed the first man on the moon
You were picking strawberries in a field,
Straggly fuses, lamps that stained the ground
And lips and fingers with reflected light,
For you were living then from hand to mouth.

Re-entering that atmosphere, you take
The dangerous bend outside the graveyard
Where your mother falls like a meteor
From clouds of may and damson blossom:
There the moon-rocks ripen in your hand.

Architecture

The House on the Seashore

Laying down sand and shingle for the floor
And thatching with seaweed the low boulders
You make an echo-chamber of your home
That magnifies the wind to a cyclone
And keeps you from standing head and shoulders
Above the sea's whisper and the seashore.

The House Shaped Like an Egg

Do you pay for this house with egg money
Since its whitewashed walls are clean as shell
And the parlour, scullery, bedrooms oval
To leave no corner for dust or devil
Or the double yolk of heaven and hell
Or days when it rains and turns out sunny?

The House on the Bleach Green

This stump of a tree without any leaves
Can be occupied but never lived in
When snow is lying on the bleach green
And the smallest house you have ever seen
Lets someone inside to watch the linen
From tiny windows with a view of thieves.

The House Made out of Turf

Are the hearth and the chimney built of stone
Or can there be a fireplace for the fire
In a house made out of turf, with its roof
Of kindling, gables that may waterproof
This spacious tinderbox to make a pyre
Of what you built and heated on your own?

The Echo Gate

I stand between the pillars of the gate,
A skull between two ears that reconstructs
Broken voices, broken stones, history

And the first words that come into my head
Echoing back from the monastery wall
To measure these fields at the speed of sound.

Ash Keys

Ghosts of hedgers and ditchers,
The ash trees rattling keys
Above tangles of hawthorn
And bramble, alder and gorse,

Would keep me from pacing
Commonage, long perspectives
And conversations, a field
That touches the horizon.

I am herding cattle there
As a boy, as the old man
Following in his footsteps
Who begins the task again,

As though there'd never been
In some interim or hollow
Wives and children, milk
And buttermilk, market days.

Far from the perimeter
Of watercress and berries,
In the middle of the field
I stand talking to myself,

While the ash keys scatter
And the gates creak open
And the barbed wire rusts
To hay-ropes strung with thorns.

Frozen Rain

I slow down the waterfall to a chandelier,
Filaments of daylight, bones fleshed out by ice
That recuperate in their bandages of glass
And, where the lake behaves like a spirit-level,
I save pockets of air for the otter to breathe.

I magnify each individual blade of grass
With frozen rain, a crop of icicles and twigs,
Fingers and thumbs that beckon towards the thaw
And melt to the marrow between lip and tongue
While the wind strikes the branches like a celeste.

Thaw

Snow curls into the coalhouse, flecks the coal.
We burn the snow as well in bad weather
As though to spring-clean that darkening hole.
The thaw's a blackbird with one white feather.

Spring Tide

1

I seem lower than the distant waves,
Their roar diluting to the stillness
Of the sea's progression across these flats,
A map of water so adjusted
It behaves like a preservative
And erases neither the cattle's
And the sheep's nor my own footprints.
I leave hieroglyphics under glass
As well as feathers that hardly budge,
Down abandoned at preening places
That last so long as grassy islands
Where swans unravel among the ferns.

2

It isn't really a burial mound
Reflected there, but all that remains
Of a sandy meadow, a graveyard
Where it was easy to dig the graves.
The spring tide circles and excavates
A shrunken ramshackle pyramid
Rinsing cleaner scapulae, tibias,
Loose teeth, cowrie and nautilus shells
Before seeping after sun and moon
To pour cupfuls into the larks' nests,
To break a mirror on the grazing
And lift minnows over the low bridge.

3
The spring tide has ferried jelly fish
To the end of the lane, pinks, purples,
Wet flowers beside the floating cow pats.
The zigzags I make take me among
White cresses and brook weed, lousewort,
Water plantain and grass of parnassus
With engraved capillaries, ivory sheen:
By a dry stone wall in the dune slack
The greenish sepals, the hidden blush
And a lip's red veins and yellow spots —
Marsh helleborine waiting for me
To come and go with the spring tide.

Lore

Cutting the Last Sheaf

Divide into three braids the thickest clump of corn
Plaiting it like hair, tying it below the ears
To make sure that the harvest will not unravel,

Then, as though to hone them sharper upon the wind
Throw sickles until the last sheaf has been severed
And give it to a woman or a mare in foal.

Fishing for Sand Eels

They are hungry enough to fish for eels,
Sand eels, except that it's hardly fishing
To parade so slowly between the tides,

To be one of the moonlit multitude,
To slice sand and sea with a blunt sickle
Lest the harvest bleed when it is cut.

Working the Womenfolk

The man who would like his wife to dig in the fields
Will have to attach a wooden peg to her hoe,
Then cover her.feet, and not with stockings only,

And do his bit at the milking stool and the churn
And even keep an eye on the wandering hen
For fear she might be laying in the nettle patch.

Bringing in the Kelp

There are even more fields under the sea
As though waves washed over a remote farm
And lanes extended there for cart or raft,

As though the handles of rake and sickle
Grew much longer in order to harvest
The salty tangle from those deep waters.

Ploughing by the Tail

Whoever plucks wool in thrifty skeins from his sheep
And bleeds his bull through a small hole in the neck
And blows into his cow to make her give more milk,

Is likely to do without a halter and reins
And plough by the tail, if the hairs are strong enough
And he has learned to tie the complicated knot.

Finding a Remedy

Sprinkle the dust from a mushroom or chew
The white end of a rush, apply the juice
From fern roots, stems of burdock, dandelions,

Then cover the wound with cuckoo-sorrel
Or sphagnum moss, bringing together verse
And herb, plant and prayer to stop the bleeding.

On Hearing Irish Spoken

Gliding together in a tidal shimmer to talk
Two fishermen leave behind another currach
Upturned on the beach, a hand cupped to an ear,

An echo of technical terms, the one I know
Repeating itself at desperate intervals
Like the stepping stones across a river in spate.

Mayo Monologues

1. Brothers

I was a mother and a father to him
Once his pebble spectacles had turned cloudy
And his walk slowed to a chair by the fire.
Often I would come back from herding sheep
Or from the post office with our pensions
To find his darkness in darkness, the turf
Shifting ashes on to last flakes of light.
The room was made more silent by the flies
That circled the soup stains on his waistcoat.
The dog preferred to curl up under his hand
And raced ahead as soon as I neared the lane.
I read to him from one of his six books,
Thick pages dropping from the broken spines
Of *Westward Ho!* and *The Children's Reciter.*
Sometimes I pulled faces, and he didn't know,
Or I paraded naked in front of him
As though I was looking in a mirror.
Two neighbours came visiting after he died.
Mad for the learning, a character, they said
And awakened in me a pride of sorts.
I picture his hand when I stroke the dog,
His legs if I knock the kettle from the hearth.
It's his peculiar way of putting things
That fills in the spaces of Tullabaun.
The dregs stewed in the teapot remind me,
And wind creaming rainwater off the butt.

2. Housekeeper

She burst out laughing at the interview
Because he complained about his catheter.
I had come from the far end of the county
To nurse his lordship and, when he died, stayed on.
Every morning here I have been surprised
By the stream that flows in the wrong direction.
I miss a mountain at the kitchen window.
The house is shrinking slowly to a few rooms
Where for longer periods she hides away
And sits arguing with herself, a hare
That chews over its droppings in the form.
I have caught her reading my letters home,
Hiding Christmas cards behind the piano.
She makes jokes to the friendly gardener
About my whiskery chin, my varicose veins,
And tells me off like a child in front of him
Should my fingernails be stained or floury.
If I start to talk about going home
She pretends not to understand my accent.
The bell that summons the afternoon tray
Will soon be ringing out for a bed pan.
Furniture and ornaments seem to linger
And wait under dust sheets for her to die.
A last sheet will cover up her armchair
And the hare that melts into the mountainside
Will be white in winter and eating snow.

3.   Self-heal

I wanted to teach him the names of flowers,
Self-heal and centaury; on the long acre
Where cattle never graze, bog asphodel.
Could I love someone so gone in the head
And, as they say, was I leading him on?
He'd slept in the cot until he was twelve
Because of his babyish ways, I suppose,
Or the lack of a bed: hadn't his father
Gambled away all but rushy pasture?
His skull seemed to be hammered like a wedge
Into his shoulders, and his back was hunched,
Which gave him an almost scholarly air.
But he couldn't remember the things I taught:
Each name would hover above its flower
Like a butterfly unable to alight.
That day I pulled a cuckoo-pint apart
To release the giddy insects from their cell.
Gently he slipped his hand between my thighs.
I wasn't frightened; and still I don't know why,
But I ran from him in tears to tell them.
I heard how every day for one whole week
He was flogged with a blackthorn, then tethered
In the hayfield. I might have been the cow
Whose tail he would later dock with shears,
And he the ram tangled in barbed wire
That he stoned to death when they set him free.

4. Arrest

The sergeant called me by my christian name
And waited an hour while I tidied up.
Not once did he mention why he had come
Or when and where he would take me away.
He just moved quietly from wall to wall
As I swept the floor towards the flagstones
And leaned brush and shovel, the broken tongs
Next to the spade and hoe I'd brought inside.
I emptied the half-used packet of tea
Into the caddy and dusted the lid.
In the leaky basin with its brown ring
I washed knife, fork, spoon, the two teacups
And the saucer that does for an ashtray.
I put back the stools where they usually stand,
Hung the towel to dry over one of them
And spread fresh newspapers on the table.
When I'd thrown the water from the basin
I turned it upside down on the turf stack,
Then I packed my shaving brush and razor
And stoored the fire as though I might return.
They have locked me up in the institute
Because I made love to the animals.
I'd sooner stand barefoot, without a cap
And take in my acres from a distance,
From the rocky hilltops or the seashore,
From the purgatory of the windy gaps.

Entomology

The Wasp's Nursery

Graduating from underground tunnels,
Woody corridors, leaves, the oak-apple
To caterpillars, whites, fritillaries,
The wasp takes over the spider as well,
One poison cancelling out the other,
The sting in the mouth, the sting in the tail.

The Dragonfly's Eye

Like a stained glass window diminished
To a prism the size of a pinhead,
The dragonfly's eye will be deflected
By its own wings, smithereens of daylight,
Molten glass spilling over the long back,
Segments of a bubble about to burst.

The Sundew's Menu

A dinner service becoming mouths
With just one snorkel above the bog,
The sundew puts out roots into the air,
Improves its hungry house by taking in
Passers-by, midges, mayflies, prisoners
Digested by their handcuffs and chains.

The Butterfly Net

To catch butterflies in a butterfly net
Is to sense the unfolding of a shroud,
Is to count the many changes of skin
And the chances of being born again,
Is to waken up after sleeping in.
Even their eggs are built with little doors.

Botany

Duckweed

Afloat on their own reflection, these leaves
With roots that reach only part of the way,
Will fall asleep at the end of summer,
Draw in their skirts and sink to the bottom.

Foxglove

Though the corolla dangles upside down,
Nothing ever falls out, neither nectar
Nor loosening pollen grains: a thimble,
Stall for the little finger and the bee.

Dock

Its green flowers attract only the wind
But a red vein may irrigate the leaf
And blossom into blush or birthmark
Or a remedy for the nettle's sting.

Orchid

The tuber absorbs summer and winter,
Its own ugly shape, twisted arms and legs,
A recollection of the heart, one artery
Sprouting upwards to support a flower.

Bog Cotton

Let me make room for bog cotton, a desert flower —
Keith Douglas, I nearly repeat what you were saying
When you apostrophised the poppies of Flanders
And the death of poetry there: that was in Egypt
Among the sandy soldiers of another war.

(It hangs on by a thread, denser than thistledown,
Reluctant to fly, a weather vane that traces
The flow of cloud shadow over monotonous bog —
And useless too, though it might well bring to mind
The plumpness of pillows, the staunching of wounds,

Rags torn from a petticoat and soaked in water
And tied to the bushes around some holy well
As though to make a hospital of the landscape —
Cures and medicines as far as the horizon
Which nobody harvests except with the eye.)

You saw that beyond the thirstier desert flowers
There fell hundreds of thousands of poppy petals
Magnified to blood stains by the middle distance
Or through the still unfocused sights of a rifle —
And Isaac Rosenberg wore one behind his ear.

The War Poets

Unmarked were the bodies of the soldier-poets
For shrapnel opened up again the fontanel
Like a hailstone melting towards deep water
At the bottom of a well, or a mosquito
Balancing its tiny shadow above the lip.

It was rushes of air that took the breath away
As though curtains were drawn suddenly aside
And darkness streamed into the dormitory
Where everybody talked about the war ending
And always it would be the last week of the war.

Peace

after Tibullus

Who was responsible for the very first arms deal —
The man of iron who thought of marketing the sword?
Or did he intend us to use it against wild animals
Rather than ourselves? Even if he's not guilty
Murder got into the bloodstream as gene or virus
So that now we give birth to wars, short cuts to death.
Blame the affluent society: no killings when
The cup on the dinner table was made of beechwood,
And no barricades or ghettos when the shepherd
Snoozed among sheep that weren't even thoroughbreds.

I would like to have been alive in the good old days
Before the horrors of modern warfare and warcries
Stepping up my pulse rate. Alas, as things turn out
I've been press-ganged into service, and for all I know
Someone's polishing a spear with my number on it.
God of my Fathers, look after me like a child!
And don't be embarrassed by this handmade statue
Carved out of bog oak by my great-great-grandfather
Before the mass-production of religious art
When a wooden god stood simply in a narrow shrine.

A man could worship there with bunches of early grapes,
A wreath of whiskery wheat-ears, and then say Thank you
With a wholemeal loaf delivered by him in person,
His daughter carrying the unbroken honeycomb.
If the good Lord keeps me out of the firing line
I'll pick a porker from the steamy sty and dress
In my Sunday best, a country cousin's sacrifice.
Someone else can slaughter enemy commanders
And, over a drink, rehearse with me his memoirs,
Mapping the camp in wine upon the table top.

It's crazy to beg black death to join the ranks
Who dogs our footsteps anyhow with silent feet —
No cornfields in Hell, nor cultivated vineyards,
Only yapping Cerberus and the unattractive
Oarsman of the Styx: there an anaemic crew
Sleepwalks with smoky hair and empty eye-sockets.
How much nicer to have a family and let
Lazy old age catch up on you in your retirement,
You keeping track of the sheep, your son of the lambs,
While the woman of the house puts on the kettle.

I want to live until the white hairs shine above
A pensioner's memories of better days. Meanwhile
I would like peace to be my partner on the farm,
Peace personified: oxen under the curved yoke;
Compost for the vines, grape-juice turning into wine,
Vintage years handed down from father to son;
Hoe and ploughshare gleaming, while in some dark corner
Rust keeps the soldier's grisly weapons in their place;
The labourer steering his wife and children home
In a hay cart from the fields, a trifle sozzled.

Then, if there are skirmishes, guerilla tactics,
It's only lovers quarrelling, the bedroom door
Wrenched off its hinges, a woman in hysterics,
Hair torn out, cheeks swollen with bruises and tears —
Until the bully-boy starts snivelling as well
In a pang of conscience for his battered wife:
Then sexual neurosis works them up again
And the row escalates into a war of words.
He's hard as nails, made of sticks and stones, the chap
Who beats his girlfriend up. A crime against nature.

Enough, surely, to rip from her skin the flimsiest
Of negligees, ruffle that elaborate hair-do,
Enough to be the involuntary cause of tears —
Though upsetting a sensitive girl when you sulk
Is a peculiar satisfaction. But punch-ups,
Physical violence, are out: you might as well
Pack your kit-bag, goose-step a thousand miles away
From the female sex. As for me, I want a woman
To come and fondle my ears of wheat and let apples
Overflow between her breasts. I shall call her Peace.

Sulpicia

Round this particular date I have drawn a circle
For Mars, dressed myself up for him, dressed to kill:
When I let my hair down I am a sheaf of wheat
And I bring in the harvest without cutting it.

Were he to hover above me like a bird of prey
I would lay my body out, his little country,
Fields smelling of flowers, flowers in the hedgerow —
And then I would put on an overcoat of snow.

I will stumble behind him through the undergrowth
Tracking his white legs, drawing about us both
The hunters' circle: among twisted nets and snares

I will seduce him, tangle his hairs with my hairs
While the stag dashes off on one of its tangents
And boars root safely along our circumference.

Florence Nightingale

Through your pocket glass you have let disease expand
To remote continents of pain where you go far
With rustling cuff and starched apron, a soft hand:
Beneath the bandage maggots are stitching the scar.

For many of the men who lie there it is late
And you allow them at the edge of consciousness
The halo of your lamp, a brothel's fanlight
Or a nightlight carried in by nanny and nurse.

You know that even with officers and clergy
Moustachioed lips will purse into fundaments
And under sedation all the bad words emerge
To be rinsed in your head like the smell of wounds,

Death's vegetable sweetness at both rind and core —
Name a weed and you find it growing everywhere.

Grace Darling

After you had steered your coble out of the storm
And left the smaller islands to break the surface,
Like draughts shaking that colossal backcloth there came
Fifty pounds from the Queen, proposals of marriage.

The daughter of a lighthouse keeper and the saints
Who once lived there on birds' eggs, rainwater, barley
And built to keep all pilgrims at a safe distance
Circular houses with views only of the sky,

Who set timber burning on the top of a tower
Before each was launched at last in his stone coffin —
You would turn your back on mainland and suitor
To marry, then bereave the waves from Lindisfarne,

A moth against the lamp that shines still and reveals
Many small boats at sea, lifeboats, named after girls.

Metamorphoses

1
A boulder locked in a cranny,
A head without a face, she waits
For rain to hollow out a font
And fill her eye in, blink by blink.

2
She will be felled like timber
So that anyone may study
Clefts made by the highest branches,
The faces hidden in the bark.

3
She sleeps in ponds and puddles
And sinks to her own level,
A bed for watercress, water
Snuggling in its own embrace.

4
Her legs are the roots of a tree
That have grown around a boulder
As though she might give birth to it
By pressing hard into the ground.

Mountain Swim

Hilltop and valley floor we sway between,
Our bodies sustained as by a hammock,
Our nakedness water stretched on stone,

One with the shepherd's distant whistle,
The hawk lifted on its thermal, the hare
Asleep in its excrement like a child.

On Mweelrea

1

I was lowering my body on to yours
When I put my ear to the mountain's side
And eavesdropped on water washing itself
In the locked bath-house of the underground.

When I dipped my hand among hidden sounds
It was the water's pulse at wrist and groin,
It was the water that reminded me
To leave all of my jugs and cups behind.

2

The slopes of the mountain were commonage
For me clambering over the low walls
To look for the rings of autumn mushrooms
That ripple out across the centuries.

I had made myself the worried shepherd
Of snipe twisting the grasses into curls
And tiny thatches where they hid away,
Of the sheep that grazed your maidenhair.

3

September grew to shadows on Mweelrea
Once the lambs had descended from the ridge
With their fleeces dyed, tinges of sunset,
Rowan berries, and the bracken rusting.

Behind my eyelids I could just make out
In a wash of blood and light and water
Your body colouring the mountainside
Like uncut poppies in the stubbly fields.

Meniscus

You are made out of water mostly, spittle, tears
And the blood that colours your cheek, red water.
Even your ears are ripples, your knuckles, knees
Damp stones that wear the meniscus like a skin.
Your breasts condense and adhere, drops of water.
And, where your body curves to a basin, faces
Are reflected, then dissolved by swaying water.

The Linen Industry

Pulling up flax after the blue flowers have fallen
And laying our handfuls in the peaty water
To rot those grasses to the bone, or building stooks
That recall the skirts of an invisible dancer,

We become a part of the linen industry
And follow its processes to the grubby town
Where fields are compacted into window-boxes
And there is little room among the big machines.

But even in our attic under the skylight
We make love on a bleach green, the whole meadow
Draped with material turning white in the sun
As though snow reluctant to melt were our attire.

What's passion but a battering of stubborn stalks,
Then a gentle combing out of fibres like hair
And a weaving of these into christening robes,
Into garments for a marriage or funeral?

Since it's like a bereavement once the labour's done
To find ourselves last workers in a dying trade,
Let flax be our matchmaker, our undertaker,
The provider of sheets for whatever the bed —

And be shy of your breasts in the presence of death,
Say that you look more beautiful in linen
Wearing white petticoats, the bow on your bodice
A butterfly attending the embroidered flowers.

Martinmas

Not even ashes and the sweepings from the floor
Are to be thrown out, stray hairs of yours, flakes of skin,
For that would be digging a grave, burying someone
Before the weather mends and cold stones are lifted
From the river bed, the charred sticks from our hearth,
My sooty finger smudging your arm and forehead
As I leave to scatter grain into the furrows,
To wait with my sickle among the unripe stalks
Until the Feast of Saint Martin, you by my bed
Letting down your hair and weeping while you undress
Because you are the harvest I must gather in.
We grind the ears of corn to death between our bones.

Household Hints

Old clothes have hearts, livers that last longer:
The veils, chemises, embroidered blouses
Brought back to life in suds and warm water,
Black lace revived by black tea, or crape
Passed to and fro through steam from a kettle.

So look on this as an antique nightdress
That has sleepwalked along hundreds of miles
Of rugs and carpets and linoleum,
Its clean hem lifted over the spilt milk
And ink, the occasional fall of soot.

This places you at a dressing-table,
Two sleeves that float into the looking-glass
Above combs and brushes, mother-of-pearl,
Tortoiseshell, silver, the discreet litter
Of your curling papers and crimping pins.

Though I picked it up for next to nothing
Wear this each night against your skin, accept
My advice about blood stains and mildew,
Cedar wood and camphor as protection
Against moths, alum-water against fire,

For I have been bruised like the furniture
And am more than a list of household hints,
The blackleader of stoves and bootscrapers,
Mender of sash cords, the mirror you slip
Between sheets to prove that the bed is damp.

The Rag Trade

You walk around Smithfield in my dream
On christian name terms with the owners
Of old clothes stalls, second-hand bookshops,

Drifting between thrift and nostalgia,
That ache to reach home before the dust's
Final version of your school stories,

Before moths flit out like a nightmare
From the sweaty arm-holes in dresses
Worn by a mother or grandmother.

I am the man wiping his windscreen
With a rag you recognise as silk
Or chiffon, perfect material,

A stray to be taken in by you,
Washed, cared for, taught the secrets
Of covering and revealing your body.

When you ask for it, I give because
My books will always be second-hand,
Your underclothes never out of fashion.

Dead Men's Fingers

The second time we meet I am waiting in a pub
Beside the cigarette machine. She is in her moons.
A cat with a mouse's tail dangling out of its mouth
Flashes from between her legs and escapes into my head.
There follow trips to the seaside where I find for her
Feathers, shells, dune violets among the marram grass;

Then the conversational strolls in a forest of pines
So that I can picture the invisible tree-creeper
Spiralling up her body to probe for such parasites
As lurk where pink flowers seem to harden into cones.
Next comes that honeymoon weekend in a farflung cottage
Where we sit in silence and borrow light from the door,

And I boil a somnolent lobster in the ash bucket
And divide it between us. Our most memorable meal.
But surely she has eaten dead men's fingers by mistake
Because her sickness interrupts us like a telephone.
The tenth, eleventh, twelfth occasions melt together
Colourfully: a stained glass window in a burning church.

Indeed, I soon find myself, wherever a fire is lit,
Crossing my legs, putting my feet up on the mantelpiece
And talking to my shoes, with glances in her direction.
The first time we meet is really the last time in reverse.
We kiss for ever and I feel like the ghost of a child
Visiting the mother who long ago aborted him.

The Barber's Wife

I seem to be the last customer
For blinds are drawn on instruments,

On combs and razors, clicking scissors,
Clippers that buzz among pomades.

As though everything depends on it
A drop of water clings to the tap,

A lens inverting the premises
Until the barber's wife appears.

Does she always come at five o'clock
To sweep the presences, absences,

Earthly remains, ghosts of skulls
With graceful movements into the bin?

She is an interloper, two eyes
Penetrating the back of my head.

Then I see that she repeats herself
In one mirror after another,

That the barber and I are eunuchs
In the harem of her reflections.

Self-portrait

My great-great-grandfather fell in top hat and tails
Across the threshold, his cigar brightly burning
While the chalk outline they had traced around his body
Got up and strolled through the door and became me,

But not before his own son had wasted a lifetime
Waiting to be made Lord Mayor of the Universe.
He was to choke to death on a difficult word
When a food particle lodged against his uvula.

I came into being alongside a twin brother
Who threatened me at first like an abortionist
Recommending suicide jumps and gin with cloves.
Then he blossomed into my guardian angel.

Peering back to the people who ploughed the Long Field
My eyes are bog holes that reflect a foreign sky.
Moustaches thatch my utterance in such a way
That no one can lipread the words from a distance.

I am, you will have noticed, all fingers and thumbs
But, then, so is the wing of a bat, a bird's wing.
I articulate through the nightingale's throat,
Sing with the vocal chords of the orang-outang.

52

Codicils

1
Your hands hold my neck and head
As though you were bathing me
Or lifting me out of darkness,
Hands that shelter a nightlight,
Balance a spoon for medicine.

When you turn from me to sleep
A lamplighter on his bicycle
Will see you to the corner,
Gas mantles in his saddle bag,
Across his shoulder a long pole.

2
It is a last desolate weaning
When you hug me, the sole survivor
— Without location or protocol —
Of a tribe which let the fire go out.

I shall explain to the first stranger
With a smattering of my dialect
Why I am huddled up in mourning
And, like a baby, sucking my thumb.

Notes

p.10: Oliver Plunkett's mummified head is kept in a glass casket on the altar of Drogheda Cathedral.

p.18: The Echo Gate is situated on the outskirts of Trim in County Meath.

p.33: The poems alluded to are *Desert Flowers* by Keith Douglas and Isaac Rosenberg's *Break of Day in the Trenches*.

p.38: Sulpicia was a Roman poet of the Augustan age. This sonnet is a collage of original lines and free translations of lines and phrases from the Latin.

p.40: A coble is a Northumbrian fishing-boat.

p.48: The reference is not to London's more famous Smithfield Market, but to the one in Belfast which was burnt down during the present troubles and rebuilt unsatisfactorily.